Lesson 31 What Do You Want to Say?
Lesson 32 What Should He Do?
Lesson 33 Agree or Disagree?
Lesson 34 Do You Believe?
Lesson 35 Priorities
Lesson 36 What Are Their Excuses?
Lesson 37 Pros. & Cons.
Lesson 38 What Would You Do?
Lesson 39 Making Choices
Lesson 40 What Are the Reasons?
Lesson 41 Right or Wrong?
Lesson 42 What Would Happen?
Lesson 43 What Is It?
Lesson 44 What Sub-Categories Are There?
Lesson 45 What's the Difference?
Lesson 46 Different Personalities
Lesson 47 What Do They Suffer?
Lesson 48 What Does This Mean? (1)
Lesson 49 What Does This Mean? (2)
Lesson 50 Proverbs
Lesson 51 Acronyms
Lesson 52 Lifestyle Quips
Lesson 53 Make Your Point (1)
Lesson 54 Make Your Point (2)
Lesson 55 Social Phenomena
Lesson 56 Who Is Responsible ...
Lesson 57 What Is Wrong ...
Lesson 58 Good Things ...
Lesson 59 What Has This ...
Lesson 60 Laughter Is ...

Introduction

LIS Korea educational products proudly presents a new version of its popular English learning series, NEW TALK, TALK, TALK. Like the other volumes produced by this innovative company, it is not concerned with grammar or vocabulary, as such, though many words and expressions are defined in context. The main purpose is for students to see and hear modern American English as used by an intelligent native speaker, and to respond with their own ideas, in their own words. Mature communication is the goal: the ability of two or more people to understand and interact with each other on an equal basis.

As usual, the NEW TALK, TALK, TALK contains many lively, interesting topics that span the range of human experience, a number of sometimes-outrageous opinions, dialogues between people with sharply different opinions and personalities, and — what is most lacking in regular language-learning texts — a great deal of good sense. It is in this last category in particular that NEW TALK, TALK, TALK and other LIS Korea products excel. Users are routinely asked to explain some word or sentence, how to use it, and what is REALLY means (not just the dictionary definition) in the context of the situation being presented. Human character and human interpretation vary widely, and so does the language used; sometimes, even the same word or phrase takes on different coloration in different settings. The material in this series is designed to help non-native-speakers navigate socially in different circumstances.

Duane L. Vorhees

머리말

영어교육 분야에서 Topic-Discussion Textbook Series 를 출간하면서 많은 독자들로부터 사랑을 받아 온 리스 코리아가 이번에 독특한 감각과 새로운 포맷을 가진 교재 New Talk Talk Talk (1/2)를 새롭게 출간하였습니다. 그 동안의 리스 코리아 교재들이 주로 중 고급 학습자들을 위한 것이었다면 이번에 출간하는 New Talk Talk Talk (1/2)는 초/중/고급 모든 학습자들을 위한 교재입니다.

New Talk Talk Talk(1/2) 교재의 특징은 다음과 같습니다.

1. 각권 30과로 구성 되었으며 각 Lesson 은 각기 다른 포맷으로 구성되어 있습니다.

2. Lesson 첫 부분에 Example 과 Answer 를 제시하여 학습자들이 각 Lesson 의 목적을 잘 이해하 게끔 배려하였습니다.

3. 특히 Book (1) 의 Part (3) "Let's Practice Making Questions" 는 새롭게 시도되는 포맷으로서 영 어 학습자들의 부족한 부분을 다시 한번 훈련하도록 특별히 제시된 부분 입니다. 그 동안에 많 은 학습자들이 선생님들의 질문에만 대답하는 훈련을 해왔습니다. 따라서 실제상황에서 질문 을 할 경우에는 많은 어려움을 느껴왔습니다. 따라서 영어 학습자들에게는 좋은 훈련재료가 될것입니다.

4. 영어학습에 있어서 말하기든 쓰기든 학습의 출발점은 영어로 생각하고 영어로 표현해보는 것 입니다. 이 책에서는 이 부분에 많은 주안점을 두어 영어를 영어로 설명하는 훈련을 할 수 있 도록 많은 재료들을 제시하여 훈련 할 수 있도록 했습니다.

5. 또한 어려운 구문이나 단어에 대해서는 각주에서 영어로된 상세한 설명을 곁들여 도움이 되도 록 했습니다.

이제 저희 리스 코리아 편집진의 노력의 산물인 New Talk Talk Talk (1/2)와 함께 독자 여러분의 영어학 습에 새로운 발전을 기대합니다. 이책이 나오기까지 집필에 애써주신 리스 코리아 편집진들, 그리고 집필과 책임감수까지 해주신 Duane L. Vorhees 씨에게 많은 감사를 드립니다. 또 좋은 삽화를 그려주 신 김기환씨, 그리고 완벽한 교정을 위해 애써주신 Neal D. Williams 씨에게도 감사를 드립니다.

리스 코리아 발행인   최 승 신

Part I What Do You Think?

Lesson 31   What Do You Want to Say?   · · · · · · · · · · · · · 10
Lesson 32   What Should He Do?   · · · · · · · · · · · · · · 16
Lesson 33   Agree or Disagree?   · · · · · · · · · · · · · · 22
Lesson 34   Do You Believe?   · · · · · · · · · · · · · · · · 28
Lesson 35   Priorities   · · · · · · · · · · · · · · · · · · · 34
Lesson 36   What Are Their Excuses?   · · · · · · · · · · · · 40
Lesson 37   Pros & Cons   · · · · · · · · · · · · · · · · · · 46
Lesson 38   What Would You Do?   · · · · · · · · · · · · · · 52
Lesson 39   Making Choices   · · · · · · · · · · · · · · · · · 58
Lesson 40   What Are the Reasons?   · · · · · · · · · · · · · 64
Lesson 41   Right or Wrong?   · · · · · · · · · · · · · · · · 70
Lesson 42   What Would Happen?   · · · · · · · · · · · · · · 74

Part II Quizzes

Lesson 43   What Is It?   · · · · · · · · · · · · · · · · · · · 78
Lesson 44   What Sub-Categories Are There?   · · · · · · · · · 82
Lesson 45   What's the Difference?   · · · · · · · · · · · · · 86
Lesson 46   Different Personalities   · · · · · · · · · · · · · · 90
Lesson 47   What Do They Suffer?   · · · · · · · · · · · · · · 96

Part III What Does This Mean?

Lesson 48   What Does This Mean? (1)   · · · · · · · · · · · 100
Lesson 49   What Does This Mean? (2)   · · · · · · · · · · · 104
Lesson 50   Proverbs   · 112
Lesson 51   Acronyms   · 118
Lesson 52   Lifestyle Quips   · · · · · · · · · · · · · · · · · 120

Part IV Make Your Point

Lesson 53   Make Your Point (1)   · · · · · · · · · · · · · · 124
Lesson 54   Make Your Point (2)   · · · · · · · · · · · · · · 130
Lesson 55   Social Phenomena   · · · · · · · · · · · · · · · 134
Lesson 56   Who Is Responsible or Who Is More Responsible?   138
Lesson 57   What Is Wrong with This Idea?   · · · · · · · · · 142
Lesson 58   Good Things and Bad   · · · · · · · · · · · · · · 146
Lesson 59   What Has This Change Brought About?   · · · · · 150
Lesson 60   Laughter Is the Best Medicine!   · · · · · · · · · 154

Book 2
Lesson 31
What Do You Want to Say?

Part I **What Do You Think?**

 xample

Many people think technology brings happiness to our lives and that time-saving machines give us more time. How would you tell folks that, on the contrary, it is new technology itself that is a main source of modern stress?

 nswer

Computers and mobile phones tie people closely to their jobs all the time, regardless of where they work. So their workload→ increases as efficiency improves. People are busier, even though they do more, but they still lack free time. The employer is getting a great deal, since he can squeeze→ more work out of the staff→ without paying more money, but the employee can no longer take a break→ to recharge his batteries→; there is no safe place to hide and relax — the Infernal→ Machine will find him wherever he goes!

→ **workload :** amount of work a person or machine is expected to do
→ **squeeze :** barely succeed at getting or doing (sth)   → **staff :** people who work for an organization
→ **break :** brief period of time during which (sb) stops an activity
→ **recharge your batteries :** rest or relax in order to get back your energy
→ **infernal:** very bad or unpleasant
→ **save (sth) for a rainy day :** save (sth), esp. money, for a time when you will need it
→ **sunscreen :** lotion you put on your skin to prevent sunburn
→ **give up on (sth) :** stop trying to do or achieve (sth)
→ **take (sth) into consideration :** remember to think about (sth) important when you are making or judgment
→ **lay (sb) off :** stop employing (sb), esp. for a period in which there is not much work to do
→ **on a leash :** under control   → **dissuade :** make (sb) decide not to do (sth)
→ **finances :** money a person, company, organization etc. has available, or the way they manage this money
→ **walk of life :** position in society (sb) has, esp. the type of job they have

What do you want to say?

1. Because of a traffic jam, you are late to work. Apologize to your boss.

2. Tell your boss you want the day off, because you have a bad cold.

3. Tell a friend why he should save money for a rainy day.

4. Your friend failed the college entrance exam. Cheer him up and advise him to try another school.

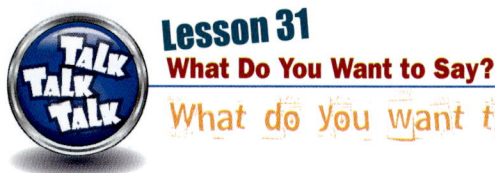

Lesson 31
What Do You Want to Say?

What do you want to say?

5. Counsel your friend to stop smoking. Tell him both why and how.

6. How would you advise one of your parents to exercise more?

7. Tell your boyfriend (or girlfriend) to be sure to carry a good sunscreen↓ on his or her summer vacation.

8. Tell your classmates not to give up on↓ English.

9. Advise your brother not to choose a job based on salary alone but to take other qualities into consideration.↓

10. Tell your friend to get a medical checkup...every year.

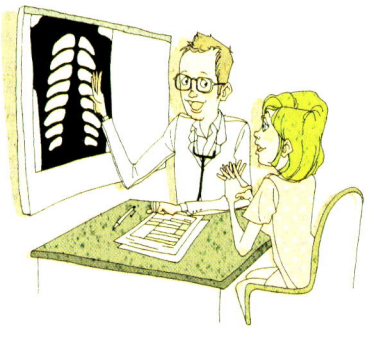

11. Explain to your children why it is important to study hard.

12. Inform your employees that it is necessary to cut their pay and to lay some of them off.↓

Lesson 31
What Do You Want to Say?

What do you want to say?

13. Let your best friend know that you won't be able to pay back his loan on time.

14. Tell your parents that you are in love and want to get married. After all, you don't think an 18-year-old is too young for marriage.

15. Tell your girlfriend or boyfriend that you have a new girlfriend/boyfriend.

16. Inform pet-people that all dogs must be kept on a leash at all times when being walked!

17. Dissuade your daughter from having a nose job.

18. Tell your wife now is the time she must go back to work, since your finances are unlikely to improve.

19. Insist that drunk drivers are potential murderers on the road, so the punishment should be stricter.

20. Argue that women are becoming more powerful in all walks of life.

Book 2
Lesson 32
What Should He Do?

▶ **Example**

He is very forgetful.

▶ **Answer**

If he forgets appointments, he needs to get in the habit of writing them down and checking his calendar regularly. If he forgets names, he should try to create a memory link between a person's appearance or position and the name — the more absurd⁺ or exotic,⁺ the easier it is to remember. If he forgets information on tests, he should stop trying to memorize everything and try to understand basic processes and relationships. We can all remember between 3 and 8 things at once, so we need to learn how to organize bigger and bigger thoughts into a small number of categories; remembering becomes very easy then. It's just a matter of training, not intelligence.

▸ **absurd :** completely stupid or unreasonable, esp. in a silly way
▸ **exotic :** very different, strange, or unusual   ▸ **flat tire :** tire with no air
▸ **suicide :** act of killing oneself
▸ **fad :** (sth) such as an interest or fashion that is very popular for a short time
▸ **on credit :** buy (sth) and pay for it later
▸ **promotion :** move to a more important job or rank in a company or organization
▸ **incentive :** (sth) that encourages (sb) to do (sth) or to work harder
▸ **inheritance :** money, property etc. that you receive from (sb) after they have died
▸ **househusband :** married man who stays at home, does cleaning, cooking, etc. and does not have another job outside the home
▸ **alibi :** claim that you cannot be guilty of a crime because you were somewhere else when the crime was committed

What should he do?

1. He has discovered that his young son has started smoking.

2. He just found out he had his pocket picked on the bus.

3. He has a flat tire‚ on the expressway.

4. He sees someone drowning.

Lesson 32
What Should He Do?

What should he do?

5. He sees someone getting ready to commit suicide.

6. He is rich and his friends keep asking for a loan.

7. His girlfriend is always on some fad diet and is getting sick as a result.

8. His wife is spending too much money on credit.

9. His son says he isn't interested in going to college.

10. For her birthday, his wife wants a diamond ring and fur coat.

11. He saw his girlfriend with another man.

12. His daughter wants to move in with her boyfriend.

Lesson 32
What Should He Do?

What should he do?

13. He has a chance for a big promotion, but if he accepts, he will have to move to another country for a long time, without his family.

14. His company is providing generous early retirement incentives.

15. He needs a new car and a new apartment, but he can't afford both at the same time.

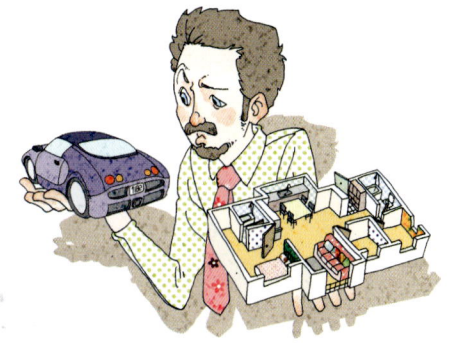

16. He is the only one among his colleagues who hasn't gotten a recent pay raise.

17. His rich father is threatening to cut off his inheritance↓ if he marries the only woman he has ever loved.

18. He lost half of his money invested in the stock market.

19. His wife wants him to be a househusband,↓ saying she has more potential for financial success.

20. His brother has committed a serious crime and needs an alibi.↓

Book 2
Lesson 33
Agree or Disagree?

▶ **E**xample

Money makes us happy.

▶ **A**nswer

If you are a miser, money makes you so happy that you never want to spend any of it. Otherwise, it is not the money that you enjoy; it is the things you can buy with it: nice vacations, comfortable homes, dressy clothes, fast cars, or new phones and computers. But the deeper question is whether material things can ever make us truly happy. Many people who seemingly have "everything" are extremely unhappy in their day-to-day dealings with the world, while many others who have "nothing" go through life with joy and gusto. True happiness is not directly related to things but, rather, to the soul.

→**miser :** (sb) who hates spending money and likes saving it
→**dressy :** formal and fashionable
→**gusto :** great enjoyment, energy, and enthusiasm
→**disgrace :** condition of feeling ashamed or losing respect or approval
→**end :** goal or purpose
→**justify :** prove or show (sth) to be just, right, or reasonable
→**means :** way of achieving a desired result
→**reverse :** opposite to what is usual
→**discriminate :** treat a person or a group differently from another in an unfair way

Agree or disagree?

1. Women are ready to do anything to look more beautiful.

2. He says life deserves to be lived for at least 100 years.

3. Marriage is the best part of a human being's life.

4. Childless couples are happier than those with kids.

Lesson 33
Agree or Disagree?
Agree or disagree?

5. Everybody lies.

6. A lot of money can break families down.

7. To die is better than to live in disgrace.

8. Animals and plants can think and feel just like us.

9. Some people treat their pets better than they treat their neighbors.

10. Love and marriage are not the same — and should not be treated alike.

11. Good looks and good brains seldom share the same body.

12. The end↓ justifies↓ the means.↓

Lesson 33
Agree or Disagree?

Agree or disagree?

13. Honesty is always the best policy.

14. Kids are getting weaker and becoming less independent all the time.

15. After 40, it's all downhill.

16. No man can be friends with any woman.

17. You can succeed if you try hard.

18. We don't have to learn any foreign languages thanks to "translating machines" that will be available in a decade.

19. Men suffer reverse⁺ discrimination⁺ in modern society.

20. To be a great artist, you have to be crazy.

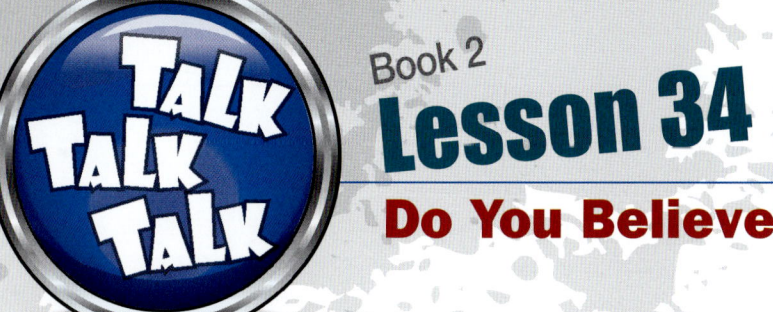

Book 2
Lesson 34
Do You Believe?

► **Example**

Do you believe in love at first sight?

► **Answer**

Absolutely not. If you think you are in love but you don't know the object of your affection very well, it's not really love. It's just infatuation↴ or lust. Love must grow with time and understanding. It requires patience and responsibility. Infatuation is a desire for an immediate relationship (usually sexual intercourse) with little or no thought about what the other person is really like.

► →**infatuation :** strong unreasonable feelings of love for (sb)
→**skeptical :** having doubts about whether (sth) is true, right, or good
→**abandon :** leave and never return to (sb)
→**figment of (sb's) imagination :** (sth) that you imagine to be real, but does not exist
→**fade away :** gradually disappear
→**destiny :** what happens in the future
→**predetermined :** decided or arranged before

Answer these questions:

1. Do you believe that how one looks affects getting a job or a promotion? Why or why not?

2. Do you believe being happy is independent of having money? Explain why or why not.

3. Do you believe the "one man/one woman" philosophy is true? Why or why not?

4. Do you believe your parents? Can you give any examples of their being right or wrong?

Lesson 34
Do You Believe?

Answer these questions:

5. Do you believe that the problems our society faces can be resolved by technology? If so, will we be happier as a result?

6. Do you believe that your kids will support you in the future? Why or why not?

7. Do you believe what ads say? Tell us why we might want to be skeptical.↓

8. Do you believe your friends will remain loyal regardless of your situation? Have any of your friends ever abandoned↓ you?

9. Do you *believe* in ghosts or are they just a figment of the imagination? Do you have any evidence for your belief?

10. Do you *believe* that money can buy anything? Name two things money can *buy* and two things it can't.

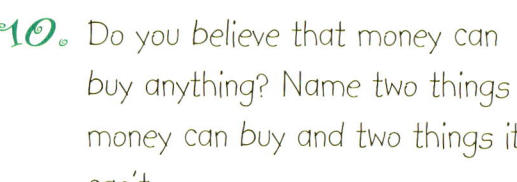

11. Do you *believe* that your love toward your sweetheart will fade away as years go by? Why or why not?

12. Do you *believe* your spouse if he or she says that he or she will not marry again after you die? Explain your answer.

Lesson 34
Do You Believe?

Answer these questions:

13. Do you believe in life after death? Why or why not?

14. Do you believe that a white lie might be a good thing in some situations? If so, when? If not, why not?

15. Do you believe the saying "the beautiful die young"? Give some examples.

16. Do you believe what salespeople say? Under what circumstances?

17. Do you believe what religious leaders say? Defend your answer.

18. Do you believe that your destiny is predetermined? What is the basis of your belief?

19. Do you believe that spanking schoolchildren has good educational effects? Explain your answer.

20. Do you believe your future will be better than your present?

Book 2
Lesson 35
Priorities

▶ **E**xample

What are your priorities↓ when you buy a car?

▶ **A**nswer

Of course, the first priority is price. I'd like to buy a cheap model with cash, so I wouldn't have to borrow any money, if possible. I'm willing to buy an old car to get the best bargain.↓ Design and make↓ are also important factors to me. And you know gas is getting expensive these days, so everybody is concerned about mileage. I like compact cars because they are economical in terms of taxes, gas, insurance, etc. Another advantage is that thieves are NEVER interested in small cars.

→**priority :** (sth) that is more important than other things and that needs to be done or dealt with first
→**bargain :** (sth) bought cheaply or for less than its usual price
→**make :** particular type of product, made by one company
→**divvy up :** divide (sth) among two or more people
→**subscribe to :** pay money, usually once a year, to have copies of a newspaper or magazine sent to you

Talk about your priorities:

1. when you choose where to honeymoon.

2. when you are looking for a girlfriend or boyfriend.

3. when you want a place to live.

4. when you decide your college major.

35

Lesson 35
Priorities

Talk about your priorities:

5. when you choose a restaurant for lunch.

6. when you are job searching.

7. when you choose where to vacation.

8. when you choose a school for your children.

9. when you divvy up↓ chores with your spouse.

10. when you subscribe to↓ a newspaper.

11. when you shop for clothes.

12. when you go drinking with your friends.

Lesson 35
Priorities

Talk about your priorities:

13. when you need a doctor.

14. when you want to change jobs.

15. when you are shopping around for insurance.

16. when you have two important events to attend, but they are at the same time.

17. when you decide on a hobby.

18. when you are in search of the perfect pet.

19. when you want to get someone a gift.

20. when you decide whether or not to emigrate.

Book 2
Lesson 36
What Are Their Excuses?

Read ME!

We hear a lot of excuses in the course of↲ our personal and social lives. Let's talk about the kinds of rationalizations↲ people often make. What are the most common excuses they make?

Example

Drivers who speed

Answer

I was in a hurry.

I didn't really notice how fast I was going.

I was late.

I was just keeping up with the flow of traffic.

I was in complete control of my car, and it is always well-maintained.

There was no danger at all.

I didn't think there would be a police officer there.

People who drive too slow are more dangerous than those who go too fast.

→in the course of (sth) : during a process or period of time
→rationalize : try to find or invent a reasonable explanation for your behavior or attitudes
→evade : avoid doing (sth) you should do according to the law
→extramarital : happening outside of a marriage
→love affair : romantic or sexual relationship, esp. between two people who are not married to each other
→ex-con : criminal who has been in prison but who is now free

What are their excuses?

1. Tax evaders.

2. Drunk drivers.

3. Divorcing couples.

4. Parents who spank their children.

Lesson 36
What Are Their Excuses?

What are their excuses?

5. People who fail to quit smoking.

6. Those who are unable to quit drinking.

7. Students who do poorly in school.

8. Politicians who don't keep their promises.

9. Men or women who have extramarital↓ love affairs.↓

10. An ex-con↓ who commits another crime.

11. Hubbies who forget their wedding anniversary.

12. Employees who are late for work.

Lesson 36
What Are Their Excuses?

What are their excuses?

13. Employers who just cut wages.

14. Students who gave up trying to learn English.

15. Singles who do not want to marry.

16. Teens who smoke and drink.

17. People who don't exercise.

18. The rich who never help the poor.

19. Young people who are constantly dieting.

20. Doctors who do not tell their patients the truth.

Book 2
Lesson 37
Pros & Cons

▶ **E**xample

You are elected president.

▶ **A**nswer

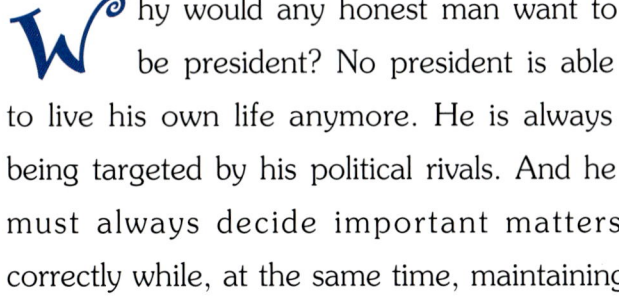

Why would any honest man want to be president? No president is able to live his own life anymore. He is always being targeted by his political rivals. And he must always decide important matters correctly while, at the same time, maintaining high moral standards. In short,⬐ his life has to be unexciting and beyond reproach⬐ if he is going to continue to hold public esteem.⬐ But sometimes he must also make deals⬐ with friends and foes⬐ alike in order to accomplish anything. But if a man has some intellectual ability and wants to serve his country, he should try to improve society if he can. Such an action deserves the respect of his fellows. And such a person could use the power of the presidency to make things better for everyone. This person would be far better than just a power-hungry politician who cares more about the benefits of office⬐ than the national welfare.

→**in short :** in a few words   →**beyond reproach :** impossible to criticize; perfect
→**esteem :** feeling of respect and admiration for (sb)   →**make deals :** make agreements
→**foe :** enemy   →**office :** important job or position with power, esp. in government
→**soap opera :** television or radio story about the daily lives of the same group of people, which is broadcast regularly
→**henpecked :** constantly controlled and criticized by his wife
→**conglomerate :** large business that is made of different kinds of companies

Talk about the advantages and disadvantages of the following:

1. You are a man.

2. You are a woman.

3. You are single.

4. You watch soap operas a lot.

Lesson 37
Pros & Cons

Talk about the advantages and disadvantages of the following:

5. You live in a big city.

6. You still live with your parents even though you are married.

7. You live with your parents-in-law.

8. You are a full-time housewife.

48

9. Your wife has a job outside the home.

10. You have won the lottery.

11. You are the oldest son.

12. You only have daughters.

Lesson 37
Pros & Cons

Talk about the advantages and disadvantages of the following:

13. You are childless.

14. You are a billionaire.

15. You are henpecked.

16. You have a car.

50

17. Your daughter in high school has a boyfriend.

18. Your kid, a college student, has several part-time jobs.

19. You own your own business.

20. You are an employee of a big conglomerate.

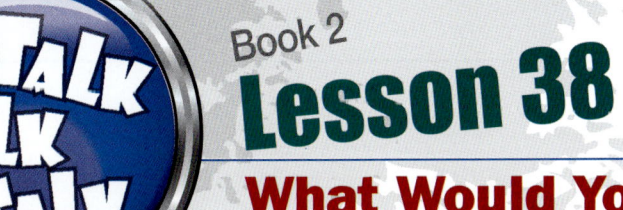

Book 2
Lesson 38
What Would You Do?

▶ **Example**

What would you do if your wife refused to live with your parents?

▶ **Answer**

First I would give her many reasons why all of us living together makes sense.↓ For example, I would tell her my parents would be around↓ all the time to help look after our children and household chores, and that they have lived through many things and would be able to give us good advice to avoid some of their problems. On the other hand, they are getting older and weaker, and more lonely, and that we have a moral responsibility to support them. But if she still rejected my reasons, I would let her live alone with our children, and I would live with my parents myself. I can't let them live alone; they need someone to take care of them. After all, they sacrificed↓ everything to bring me up,↓ and now it's my turn↓ to help them.

▶
→**make sense :** have a clear meaning; easy to understand
→**around :** existing or available   →**sacrifice :** give up (sth) that is important to you
→**bring up :** educate and care for a child until they are grown up
→**turn :** chance to do (sth)
→**black eye :** darkness of the skin around your eye, because you have been hit
→**break up :** stop being together
→**snore :** breathe in a loud way through your mouth and nose while you are sleeping
→**urge :** strong wish or need   →**Doomsday :** last day of the Earth's existence

What would you do?

1. if your husband came home
drunk every night?

2. if your children fell behind in their
schoolwork?

3. if your teenage son started
smoking and drinking?

4. if you saw someone with a flat
tire on the road?

Lesson 38
What Would You Do?

What would you do?

5. if you heard someone shout, "Stop, thief"?

6. if you saw money fall from someone's bag?

7. if your child got a black eye↓ from a classmate?

8. if you got too much change back at a store?

9. if your spouse wanted you to get life insurance?

10. if you failed to get promoted twice?

11. if your sweetheart wanted to break up↓ with you?

12. if you were standing in line and an old woman cut in?

Lesson 38
What Would You Do?

What would you do?

13. if you saw a naked person at the beach?

14. if your spouse snored↓ a lot at night?

15. if you and your best friend both loved the same person?

16. if your grown-up kid didn't want to get married but wanted to live in your house?

17. if your spouse suddenly got the urge↕ to quit his or her job and take a round-the-world trip?

18. if you had to choose between your job and your marriage? [You have a very dangerous job and you know your spouse wouldn't like it.]

19. if the doctor told you that you had an incurable disease?

20. if you knew Doomsday↕ would come next year?

Book 2
Lesson 39
Making Choices

▶ **Example**

Suppose your child were spanked in school. Would you protest to the school authorities or act as though nothing happened?

▶ **Answer**

If your life message for your children is that might↓ makes right, then by all means↓ you should support corporal punishment↓ in school. Otherwise, you should make your opposition to it very clear. After all, spanking is an act of violence regardless of who does it. Teachers should not be allowed to engage in such barbaric↓ behavior. We all know violence has no positive educational value; it just begets↓ more violence. But when authority figures↓ commit violence, it seems to send the inappropriate message that sometimes it is acceptable — especially when it is performed by the strong upon the weak.

→ **might :** strength and power
→ **by all means :** of course
→ **corporal punishment :** way of officially punishing (sb) by hitting them, esp. in schools and prisons
→ **barbaric :** very cruel and violent
→ **beget :** cause (sth) or make it happen
→ **figure :** (sb) who is important in a particular way
→ **be reincarnated :** be born again in another body after you have died

Make a choice and tell why:

1. Will you get married or remain single?

2. If you were stopped for a traffic violation, would you accept the ticket or make excuses?

3. Your hubby is unable to support your family. Will you get a job yourself or simply seek a divorce?

4. Will you take your next vacation here or abroad?

Lesson 39
Making Choices

Make a choice and tell why:

5. You are going to make a trip to Busan. Will you take the express bus, the train, or a plane? Or will you drive?

6. Would you give your seat to a young child standing on the bus or keep sitting in it yourself?

7. Would you rather live in an apartment or a house?

8. Do you prefer to use the escalator or the elevator if you have a choice, or to use the steps?

9. Which do you like better, a dog
or a cat?

10. Who is more important, your
parent or your spouse?

11. Do you prefer going to the
movie theater or watching
movies on TV?

12. Do you want a son or a
daughter as your first child?

Lesson 39
Making Choices

Make a choice and tell why:

13. Would you remarry or remain single if your spouse died?

14. What do you like to drive more, a compact car or a luxury sedan?

15. Where do you usually meet your friends? A coffee shop, a bookstore, a fast-food restaurant, a park? Why?

16. Do you like beef or pork better?

17. Which do you like better:
makkoli, soju, beer, or whiskey?

18. What would you choose for
breakfast: cereal with milk or
a traditional Korean dish?

19. Do you want your baby to be
breast-fed or bottle-fed?

20. Do you want to be reborn
[reincarnated]↓ as a man or
a woman?

Book 2
Lesson 40
What Are the Reasons?

▶ **E**xample

We study history in school. Why?

▶ **A**nswer

The most popular reason given is that we can learn from our past mistakes. But any serious study of history shows that we don't learn much — we keep doing the same dumb⁺ things time and time again. This is true even though, broadly speaking,⁺ the same circumstances occur again and again. So the real reasons we should take history seriously is to gain a deeper understanding of human activity at large,⁺ and to give ourselves some sort of identity as part of a larger entity⁺ such as a nation or culture that has traditions and roots.

▶ →**dumb :** stupid   →**broadly speaking :** speaking in a general way
→**at large :** as a whole   →**entity :** (sth) that exists as a single and complete unit
→**extraterrestrial :** living creature that people think may live on another planet
→**reluctant :** slow and unwilling
→**divulge :** give (sb) information, esp. about (sth) secret
→**appeal :** quality that causes (sb) to like (sb/sth)
→**means :** method, system, object, etc. that you use as a way of achieving a result
→**naughty :** behaving badly, used esp. to describe a child who does not behave properly or obey
           a parent, teacher, etc.
→**fade away :** become weaker
→**the handicapped :** people who are physically or mentally handicapped

What are the reasons?

1. People are getting fatter. Why?

2. People aren't saving much money anymore. Why?

3. People are getting married at older ages. Why?

4. We require our leaders to have good morals. Why?

Lesson 40
What Are the Reasons?

What are the reasons?

5. Every country has laws. Why?

6. We study philosophy. Why?

7. We exercise. Why?

8. We need recreation. Why?

9. We want to find out if extraterrestrials↓ exist. Why?

10. Many people have a religion. Why?

11. One man: one woman. Why?

12. People want to travel. Why?

Lesson 40
What Are the Reasons?

What are the reasons?

13. Politicians are seldom trusted. Why?

14. Some people just want to be seen on television or have their names in the papers. Why?

15. The older people are, the more reluctant↓ they are to divulge↓ their true age. Why?

16. College degrees have lost some of their appeal.↓ Why?

17. They say stress can be the best means↓ for accomplishing something. Why?

18. Kids are becoming naughtier.↓ Why?

19. Love usually fades away...↓ as time goes by. Why?

20. The handicapped↓ have more will power than ordinary people. Why?

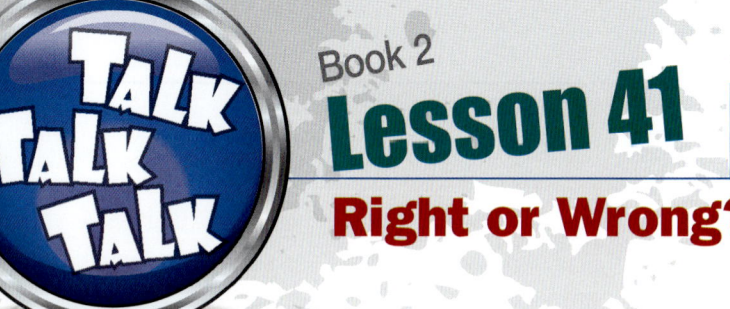

Book 2

Lesson 41

Right or Wrong?

▶ **E**xample

Money makes people happy.

▶ **A**nswer

I could never understand what people have against money. They say, for example, "Money can't buy you love." Of course it can't! But it allows you to get an education that lets you get a good job which makes it possible for you to afford to take a desirable woman on an interesting date — and allows you to have something intelligent to talk about. It lets you buy good clothes and a nice car and a home, all of which will help impress↓ her with your financial stability, so she won't have to worry so much about her children's future. And, if none of this is enough, you can flatter↓ her by giving her expensive presents. None of these activities constitute↓ "love" itself, but they all represent important steps in the process of achieving that goal. Don't you think it's better to have money in order to have a decent↓ chance to win the heart of the one you love than to lose your true love for lack of ready cash?↓

➔**impress :** affect (sb), esp. by making them feel admiration and respect for you
➔**flatter :** cause (sb) to feel pleased ➔**constitute :** make up or form (sth)
➔**decent :** good enough ➔**ready cash :** money you can spend immediately
➔**prevail :** be usual, common, or popular
➔**platonic :** having a close relationship in which there is no romance or sex
➔**nothing but :** only

Is it right or wrong?
(If so, why? If not, why not?)

1. Justice always prevails.

2. The more we know about the world, the more stress we have.

3. Of course, platonic friendship is possible between men and women!

4. Marriage is nothing but the loss of freedom.

5. Parents love us unconditionally.

Lesson 41
Right or Wrong?

Is it right or wrong? (If so, why? If not, why not?)

6. A man with a religion is happier than a man without religion.

7. A college diploma is necessary for getting a good job.

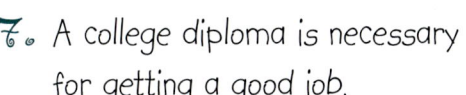

8. Environmental problems can be solved by technology.

9. A love match guarantees happiness better than an arranged marriage.

10. We don't know what happiness is until we're married.

11. It is better to have loved and lost than never to have loved at all.

12. Rich celebrities are certainly happy; why wouldn't they be?

13. All men are created equal.

14. Divorce is better than unhappiness.

15. A friend in need is a friend indeed.

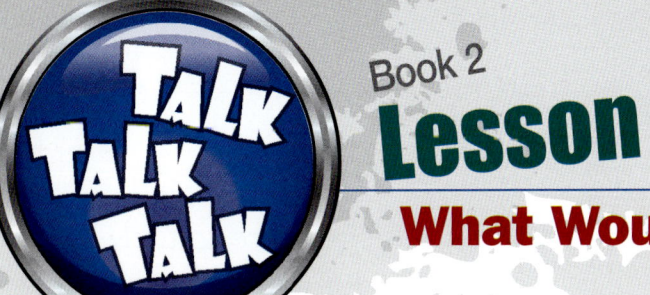

Book 2

Lesson 42

What Would Happen?

Example

Many people are calling for the abolition⁺ of the death penalty. They say capital punishment does not bring down crime rates. What would happen if their demand were accepted?

Answer

In fact, many countries have already done away with⁺ capital punishment.⁺ The odd thing is that it does not seem to make any difference at all. The various kinds

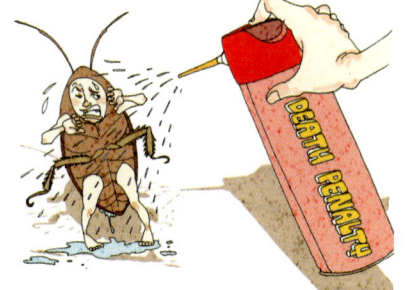

of crimes committed in any given society remain fairly constant. If murder is common before the death penalty is removed, murder rates continue at about the same pace. If kidnapping is very rare, its occurrence does not suddenly increase just because the death penalty is removed. The opposite is also true: Adding a death penalty for various crimes does not significantly⁺ deter⁺ the commission of those crimes. What we need to understand is this: laws need to be fairly and effectively enforced to keep crime rates low, but the actual nature of the punishment doesn't seem to make much difference.

→**abolish :** officially end a law, system etc., esp. one that has existed for a long time
→**do away with :** get rid of (sth)   →**capital punishment :** punishment by death
→**significantly :** in an important way or to a large degree   →**deter :** stop (sth) from happening
→**unabated :** continuing without becoming any weaker or less violent
→**consume :** eat or drink (sth)   →**mandatory :** required by a law or rule
→**adulterer :** married person who has sex with (sb) who is not that person's wife or husband

What would happen?

1. Tobacco and alcohol problems are to blame for many diseases and crimes. Their bad effects are sometimes even compared with drug problems. So what do you think would happen if the government doubled the price of liquor and cigarettes?

2.

These days many young couples choose to remain childless, claiming they are too busy to properly take care of kids or that having and raising babies is too expensive. What would happen if this trend goes unabated?

3. If people continue to consume more and more junk food (or instant food), what will happen?

Lesson 42
What Would Happen?

What would happen?

4. Many people don't like politicians, most of whom happen to be men. What do you think: would electing a female president lead to higher trust for government officials?

5. If there were no mandatory retirement age in the workplace, what would happen? Who would benefit and who would lose?

6. What would happen if the global computer system broke down, including the Internet?

7. What would happen if English became an official language in this country? Would it cause an improvement in English ability for most people?

8. All workers seem tired and under heavy stress these days. What would happen if they worked only four days a week? Do you think more leisure time would help improve productivity?

9. Current laws are said to be much too permissive. What do you think about making them stricter? For instance, what about sending drunk drivers to jail for very long periods of time? And, would there be any bad side effects?

10. What would happen if adulterers⁺ did not have to worry about going to prison?

Book 2
Lesson 43
What Is It?

Part II — **Quizzes**

▶ **Example**

The slow increase in the temperature of the Earth caused partly by the greenhouse effect↓ increasing the amount of carbon dioxide in the atmosphere.↓

▶ **Questions**

1. What is it?

2. What are the causes of this phenomenon?

▶ **Answer**

1. Global warming

2. Most climatologists↓ are convinced that a number of factors may be at work↓ but that the main contributor↓ is the vast increase in the use of carbon fuels, such as gasoline and coal. Other factors may include long-term cyclical patterns that we can do very little about. But we can do something about the main cause: use less energy or develop new sources such as solar-, nuclear-, hydrogen-, air-, thermal-, or electric-powered devices. In fact, the same climatologists are saying we must do so, very quickly, or the resultant↓ weather changes will be catastrophic.↓

→**greenhouse effect :** gradual warming of the air surrounding the Earth as a result of heat being trapped by pollution
→**the atmosphere :** mixture of gases that surrounds the Earth
→**climatology :** scientific study of climates   →**at work :** having a particular influence or effect
→**contributor :** (sth) that helps to make (sth) happen
→**resultant :** happening or existing as a result of (sth)
→**catastrophe :** terrible event in which there is a lot of destruction or many people are injured or die
→**trigger :** make (sth) happen

Answer these questions:

1. A container filled with objects typical of a particular time and place that is buried and scheduled for recovery at some particular time in the future.

▶ **Questions**

1. What is it?
2. Why would people bury one of these?

2. A very large wave or series of waves caused when something such as an earthquake moves a large quantity of water in the sea.

▶ **Questions**

1. What is it?
2. What happens when it occurs?

3. The right to remain in another country if you cannot live safely in your own because of the political situation there.

▶ **Questions**

1. What is it?
2. Who seeks it?

4. A means of providing for the nation's defense by requiring military service from certain people.

▶ **Questions**

1. What is it?
2. Is it fair, proper, or necessary?

Lesson 43
What Is It?

Answer these questions:

5. The global football (soccer) championship held every four years.

▸ **Questions**

1. What is it?
2. How important is international sports in a country's development?

6.

One means of persuading people to buy certain products or services, especially via the media.

▸ **Questions**

1. What is it?
2. How do we know if its claims are true?

7. A political act of killing as many opponents as possible by blowing oneself up in a crowded place.

▸ **Questions**

1. What is it?
2. What triggers⁺ this?

8.

The practice of promoting one nation's own industry by discouraging foreign competition, especially by charging very high tariffs.

▸ **Questions**

1. What is it?
2. Is it good for the world economy?

9. An agreement made by a man and woman *before* they marry about how they will divide their money and property if they get divorced.

▶ **Questions**

1. What is it?
2. Would you make one? Why or why not?

10.

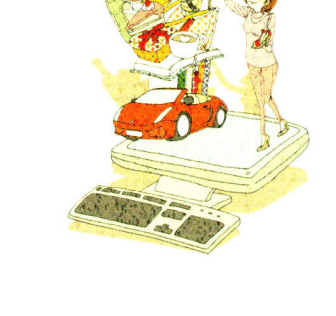

A type of diary on a *website* that is changed regularly, to give the latest news. The page usually contains someone's personal opinions, comments, and experiences.

▶ **Questions**

1. What is it?
2. Do you have one? What do you usually write?

11. The feeling that a person gets who resides in a foreign land but has trouble adapting to daily living conditions.

▶ **Questions**

1. What is it?
2. Explain what you have experienced.

12.

A cosmic *ball* of frozen gas that emits visible particles as it is *struck by* sunlight.

▶ **Questions**

1. What is it?
2. Are you afraid of the deep impact a future big comet would eventually bring about?

Book 2
Lesson 44
What Sub-Categories Are There?

▶ **Example**

Q1) What kinds of crimes are there?

Q2) What do you think is the most heinous↓ crime?

▶ **Answer**

1. Muggings,↓ fraud,↓ vandalism,↓ and murder are only a few of the many criminal offenses.

2. The worst crime is torture,↓ I think. It destroys victims' minds as well as their bodies. It makes people confess to things they are innocent of and forces them to abandon↓ their most deeply cherished principles. Even if people survive torture, its effects stay with them their entire lives. Rape is another heinous crime we often overlook.↓ It demolishes↓ a woman's (and sometimes, also, a man's) self-respect; and society often blames the victims of rape, rather than the rapists themselves, making the consequences even worse.

▶

→**heinous :** very shocking and immoral
→**mugging :** act of attacking and robbing (sb)
→**fraud :** crime of using dishonest methods to take (sth) valuable from another person
→**vandalism :** act of deliberately destroying or damaging property
→**torture :** act of deliberately hurting (sb) in order to force them to tell you (sth), to punish them, or to be cruel
→**abandon :** decide that you do not believe in a particular idea or principle anymore
→**overlook :** not notice (sth)
→**demolish :** damage (sth) so that it cannot be repaired

Answer these questions:

1.

Q1) List the kinds of weather.

Q2) What kind of weather do you like the most?

2.

Q1) What kinds of fruits are there?

Q2) Which do you like best?

3.

Q1) What kinds of music are there?

Q2) Which do you enjoy the most?

4.

Q1) What kinds of movies are there?

Q2) Which do you like the most?

Lesson 44
What Sub-Categories Are There?

Answer these questions:

5.

Q1) What kinds of professional sports are played throughout the world?

Q2) What players make the most money?

6.

Q1) List the traffic rules drivers break most often.

Q2) Which of these are the most dangerous to break?

7.

Q1) What kinds of careers exist?

Q2) What is the best profession? What is the worst?

8.

Q1) What kinds of cars are there?

Q2) What kind of car do you want? Why?

9.

Q1) List a few common diseases.

Q2) What disease are you most afraid of? Which one threatens mankind most dreadfully?

10.

Q1) What kinds of TV shows are popular?

Q2) Which night has the *best* television shows? Name them.

11.

Q1) Classify "personality."

Q2) Define your own personality type.

12.

Q1) List a few common hobbies. What are the most unusual ones?

Q2) What hobbies do you have?

Book 2
Lesson 45
What's the Difference?

Read ME!

Students are sometimes confused by similar words. Let's talk about how their real meanings differ.

Example

Public relations (PR) and advertising

Answer

PR is often called "spin." It is an attempt to promote a good public image for a person or company, especially one that may be considered controversial. But ads, quite simply, are designed to sell goods or services, rather than create an image. (Some ads attempt to do both at the same time.)

→controversial : causing a lot of disagreement

What's the difference?

1. Running and jogging

2. Tap water and bottled water

3. Being thrifty and being stingy

4. Weather and climate

Lesson 45
What's the Difference?

What's the difference?

5. Sports and exercise

6. Biography and autobiography

7. Fired and laid off

8. Aptitude and ability

9. Newspaper and magazine

10. Commercials and ads

11. Fiction and nonfiction

12. Social drinker and alcoholic

Book 2
Lesson 46
Different Personalities

Read ME!

People have different personalities, and hence they have different attitudes toward the same thing. Talk about these differences in the following cases.

Example

Those who live in the city and those who live in the country

Answer

Many people live in the city because they have to, for school or employment. But some would rather live in a rural area. City life is hectic,⁺ impersonal,⁺ noisy, and expensive. Country life is more relaxed, and people know each other better. But there is not as much to do there, and basic amenities⁺ such as emergency medical services may be difficult to obtain.

→ **hectic :** very busy or full of activity
→ **impersonal :** not showing any feelings of sympathy, friendliness etc.
→ **amenity :** (sth) that makes life easier or more pleasant
→ **law-abiding :** respectful of the law and obeying it
→ **monogamy :** custom of being married to only one person at a time
→ **goldbricker :** (sb) who stays away from their work, and esp. uses false excuses such as that they are sick
→ **couch potato :** (sb) who spends a lot of time sitting and watching television
→ **gourmet :** (sb) who knows a lot about food and wine and who enjoys good food and wine

How do they differ?

1. Buyers and non-buyers of lottery tickets

2. Those who drive safely and those who drive recklessly

3. Those who make money in the stock market and those who lose it all

4. Those who are successful in their job and those who are not

Lesson 46
Different Personalities

How do they differ?

5. Those who lead a happy life and those who do not

6. Rich people and poor ones

7. Optimists and pessimists

8. Leaders and followers

9. Those who quit smoking and those who cannot

10. Criminals and law-abiding♦ people

11. Liars and honest folks

12. Playboys and the monogamous.♦

Lesson 46
Different Personalities
How do they differ?

13. Hard workers and goldbrickers

14. Good students and poor students

15. The physically active and couch potatoes

16. Tourists and stay-at-homes

94

17. Readers and television watchers

18. Lovers of fast food and gourmets

19. Fans of pop music and of classical music

20. Ordinary sportsmen and those who pursue "extreme" sports

Book 2
Lesson 47
What Do They Suffer?

▶ **ℛead ME!**

Everybody suffers from some kind of stress. And stress differs from job to job and among personality types. Let's talk about what some real stresses are.

▶ **Ɛxample**

What kind of stress does the president probably suffer from?

▶ **Ꭿnswer**

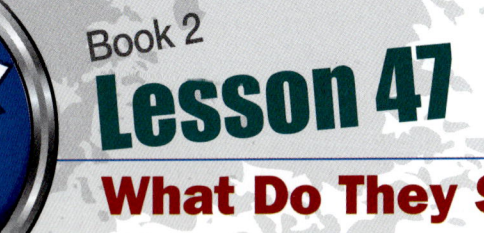

The president has to balance the needs and desires of all the sectors that make up a nation. He or she can't make all the people satisfied all the time but is under immense⁺ pressure to do so.

Some phenomena are probably beyond the ability of political leaders to deal with in an effective, direct manner (such as the weather and economic conditions), but nonetheless, the president will usually be the object of praise or scorn,⁺ depending upon the circumstances.

→**immense :** extremely large
→**scorn :** strong criticism
→**panhandle :** ask strangers for money in a public place

What are their common stresses?

1. Panhandlers

2. Cab drivers

3. Professional athletes

4. Movie stars

5. CEOs

Lesson 47
What Do They Suffer?

What are their common stresses?

6. The jobless

7. The poor

8. The rich

9. Teens

10. Retirees

11. Husbands

12. Wives

13. Students

14. Teachers

15. Ex-cons

Book 2
Lesson 48
What Does This Mean? (1)

Part III — *What Does This Mean?*

▶ **Example**

Backseat driver

▶ **Answer**

A passenger who constantly gives the driver unwanted advice, warnings, and criticism. Backseat drivers often make the driver irritated and nervous, making a traffic accident more likely. So, when you are riding in a car with someone else, you're better off remaining silent and letting him do the actual driving, even if you think he isn't doing a very good job.

Explain what these words mean:

1. Defensive driver

2. Peer pressure

3. Cheapskate

4. Big mouth

5. Clock watcher

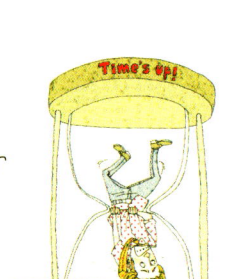

Lesson 48
What Does This Mean? (1)
Explain what these words mean:

6. Junk food

7. Mama's boy

8. Yuppie

9. Dutch treat

10. Henpecked husband

11. Runaway car

12. Junk mail

13. Stalker

14. Gold digger

15. Crocodile tears

Book 2
Lesson 49
What Does This Mean? (2)

▶ **E**xample

It's a kind of spiritual snobbery↓ that makes people think they can be happy without money.

▶ **A**nswer

This means that some people are proud to claim they don't need money to be happy. But they are not really happy; they are only trying to pretend↓ that they are. Actually, they have no ability to make money themselves and are too poor to recognize how money actually helps make people happy.

→ **snobbery :** the behavior or attitude of people who think they are better than other people
→ **pretend :** behave as if (sth) is true when you know it is not
→ **chances are :** it is likely
→ **episode :** event
→ **lean :** not having much money
→ **compromise :** agreement that is achieved after everyone involved accepts less than they wanted at first
→ **approbation :** official praise or approval
→ **bribe :** money or gifts that you give (sb) to persuade them to do (sth), esp. (sth) dishonest
→ **rein :** control
→ **inconceivable :** too strange or unusual to be thought real or possible
→ **grumble :** complain in a quiet but slightly angry way
→ **temporary :** continuing for only a limited period of time
→ **mess :** situation that is very complicated or difficult to deal with
→ **apathy :** feeling of not being interested or not caring
→ **settle :** make a final decision about (sth)
→ **affirmative :** saying or showing that the answer is "yes" rather than "no"

Explain what these sentences mean:

1. Nobody can give you wiser advice than yourself.

2. Give, and you may keep your friend even if you lose your money; lend, and the chances are↓ that you will lose your friend even if you get your money back.

3. Blessed is he who expects nothing, for he shall never be disappointed.

4. Love is the whole history of a woman's life, but just an episode↓ in a man's.

Lesson 49
What Does This Mean? (2)

Explain what these sentences mean:

5. A lean⁺ compromise⁺ is better than a fat lawsuit.

6. When asking for advice, we actually want approbation.⁺

7. Your standing in the community is established by what people say behind your back.

8. The borrower is servant to the lender.

9. A woman's beauty is not a gift to man — only a bribe.↓

10. It takes a loose rein↓ to keep a marriage tight.

11. Some people seldom repeat gossip the way they heard it.

12. A marriage without conflict is almost as inconceivable↓ as a nation without crisis.

Lesson 49
What Does This Mean? (2)

Explain what these sentences mean:

13. You can make more friends in a month by being interested in them than in ten years by trying to get them interested in you.

14. Children have more need of models than of critics.

15. It is an error to suppose that courage means bravery in everything.

16. Some people are always grumbling because roses have thorns. I am thankful that thorns have roses.

17. Adolescence is like a house on moving day — a temporary↓ mess.↓

18. I find television very educational. Every time somebody turns on the set I go into another room and read a book.

19. The opposite of love is not hate; it's apathy.↓

20. When a man says money can do anything, that settles↓ it; he doesn't have any.

Lesson 49
What Does This Mean? (2)

Explain what these sentences mean:

21. There are two kinds of failures: those who thought and never did, and those who did and never thought.

22. There is no failure except in no longer trying.

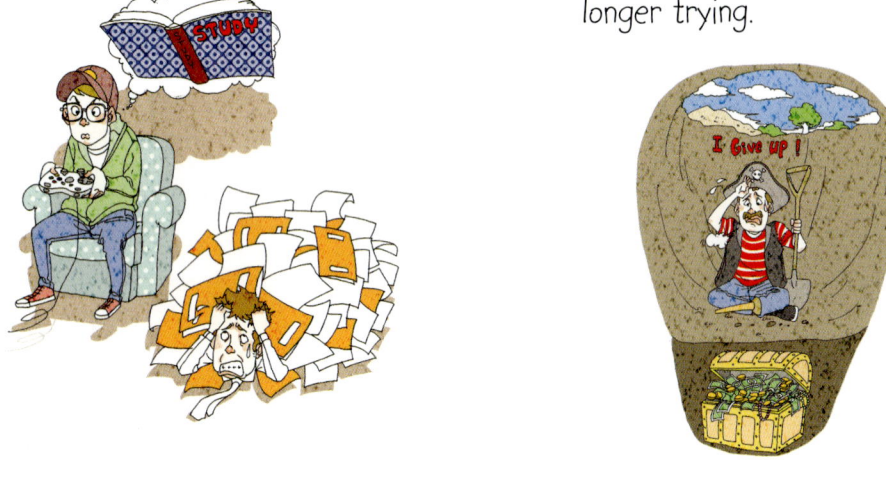

23. Some people merely ask "Why?" and others demand to know "Why not?"

24. A sure route to humiliation is to admit that you paid what the car dealer was asking.

25. The time to stop talking is when the other person nods affirmatively· but says nothing.

Book 2
Lesson 50
Proverbs

▶ **Example**

Beauty is only skin-deep.

▶ **Answer**

Something that is skin deep is shallow⁺ and superficial.⁺ It doesn't extend very far. To say "Beauty is only skin-deep" implies⁺ that something has a pretty exterior, but that's about all. What you don't see is hidden under the skin, and it may be more important than physical beauty.

▶
→ **shallow :** not deep
→ **superficial :** concerned only with what is obvious or apparent; not thorough or complete
→ **imply :** suggest that (sth) is true without saying or showing it directly
→ **get even :** harm (sb) just as much as they have harmed you
→ **venture :** risk
→ **on your feet :** honorably
→ **on your knees :** in disgrace
→ **curse :** swear

Explain what these sayings mean:

1. Easy come, easy go.

2. Don't get mad; get even.

3. Man does not live by bread alone.

4. Money talks.

5. Actions speak louder than words.

Lesson 50
Proverbs

Explain what these sayings mean:

6. A man is Known by the company he Keeps.

7. Money begets money.

8. Nothing ventured, nothing gained.

9. A rolling stone gathers no moss.

10. The shoemaker's Kids always go barefoot.

11. That's life.

12. Time will tell.

13. Every man is his own worst enemy.

14. You can't please everybody.

15. One man's trash is another man's treasure.

Lesson 50
Proverbs

Explain what these sayings mean:

16. It is better to die on your feet↓ than live on your knees.↓

17. There is no such thing as a free ride.

18. It is better to light one candle than to curse↓ the darkness.

19. Everybody's business is nobody's business.

20. If you don't make mistakes you don't make anything.

116

21. Guns don't kill people; people do.

22. The grass is always greener on the other side of the fence.

23. Money doesn't grow on trees.

24. Love is blind.

25. Do as I say, not as I do.

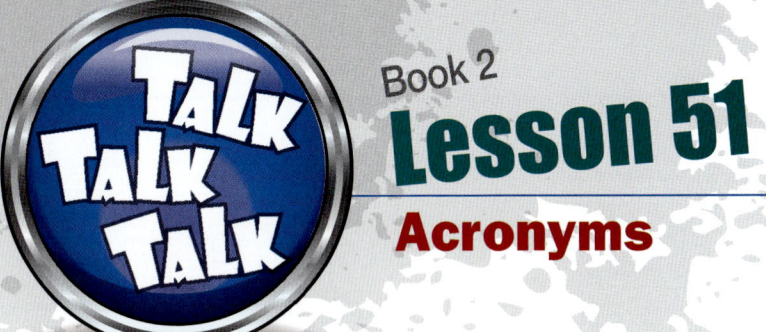

Book 2
Lesson 51
Acronyms

▶ **E**xample

FDA

Q1) What does it mean?
Q2) What does it do and how does it affect other countries' industries?

▶ **A**nswer

A1) Food and Drug Administration

A2) It tests the safety and purity of drugs and food. Countries' goods that do not meet the minimum requirements⁺ will not be allowed to enter the US for sale.

→ **requirement :** (sth) that is needed or asked for
→ **fearsome :** very frightening
→ **qualification :** skill, personal quality, or type of experience that makes you right for a particular job or position

Answer these questions:

1. UNICEF

Q1) What does it mean?

Q2) What does it do?

2. AIDS

Q1) What does it mean?

Q2) Why is it one of the most fearsome♦ diseases?

3. CEO

Q1) What does it mean?

Q2) Talk about the qualifications♦ for becoming one.

4. IMF

Q1) What does it mean?

Q2) What does it do?

5. GMO

Q1) What does it mean?

Q2) Are they safe? Why do people worry about it?

Book 2
Lesson 52
Lifestyle Quips

▶ **Example**

Even water tastes bad when taken on doctor's orders.

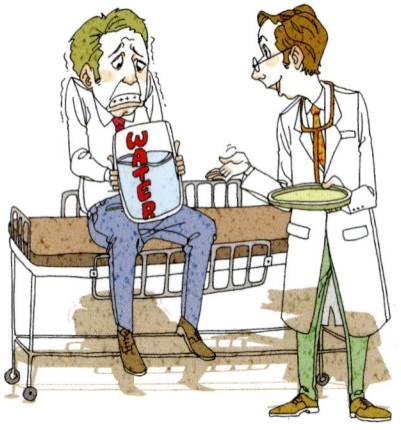

▶ **Answer**

This means that being forced to do something takes the pleasure away from that activity. I have read many good books in my life, but none of them were forced upon me by a teacher. As my boss always says, business trips are not pleasure trips. I have been around the world and visited many cities for my company, but I have not enjoyed any of them nearly as much as when I've had the time and inclination to explore one on my own. We do what we have to do, but that doesn't mean we'll like it.

→ inclination : desire to do (sth)
→ hole in one : score of one on a hole in golf
→ appreciate : be grateful
→ eternal : continuing forever
→ destination : place (sb) is going to
→ transform : completely change the appearance, form, or character of (sth)

Explain what these quips mean:

1. A mistake is proof that someone was at least trying to accomplish something.

2. Having money and friends is easy. Having friends and no money is an accomplishment.

3. Ability will enable a man to get to the top, but it takes character to keep him there.

4. Man blames most accidents on fate but feels personally responsible when he makes a hole in one.

Lesson 52
Lifestyle Quips

Explain what these quips mean:

5. Every accomplishment, great or small, starts with the right decision: "I'll try."

6. Advice is never appreciated.↓ If it leads to a good result, the recipient thinks it was his own idea; and if it turns out bad, he eternally↓ blames the advisor.

7. Ambition without determination has no destination.↓

8. A wealthy bachelor is someone who saved money to get married, and then changed his mind.

9. Maybe money can't buy love, but it can rent it.

10. The worst boss anyone can have is a bad habit.

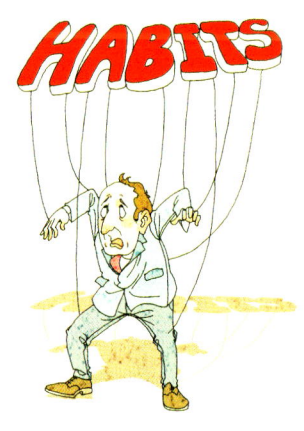

11. Wisdom is knowing the difference between determination to transform↓ those conditions which can be changed, and acceptance of those which cannot.

12. She is a woman with a past — but that doesn't stop her from looking for a man with a future!

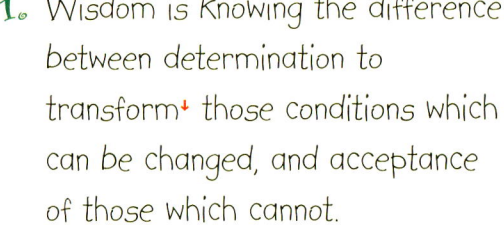

Book 2
Lesson 53
Make Your Point (1)

Part IV   *Make Your Point*

▶ **Read ME!**

Based on the outline provided, expand on the topic and give us your opinion in detail.

▶ **Example**

* Health is the most important thing in life.
* Once it is lost, you can never get it back completely.
* Be sure to eat well, sleep enough, and avoid stress if possible.
* Exercise also helps you remain fit.↓
* Regular checkups are indispensable↓ too.

→ **fit :** healthy and strong, esp. because you exercise regularly
→ **indispensible :** extremely important and necessary
→ **recoup :** get back; recover
→ **pace yourself :** do (sth) at a steady speed so that you do not get tired quickly
→ **keep in perspective :** not get too worried about
→ **work out :** exercise
→ **brisk :** quick and full of energy
→ **skyrocket :** increase suddenly and greatly
→ **rot :** have a bad effect on
→ **blood transfusion :** process of putting blood into (sb's) body as a medical treatment
→ **prejudiced :** having an unfair of dislike for (sb)
→ **obesity :** condition of being too fat in a way that is dangerous to your health
→ **fatal :** having a very bad effect
→ **innocent :** not deserving to be harmed
→ **disgust :** make (sb) feel very annoyed and upset
→ **indifferent :** not interested in
→ **triumph :** gain a victory or success
→ **vicious circle :** repeating situation or condition in which one problem causes another problem that makes the first problem worse
→ **locomotive :** powerful force that makes other things happen or succeed
→ **stimulate :** encourage or help an activity to begin or develop further
→ **uncertainty :** quality of not being sure or of feeling doubt about what will happen

Make your point (you may also disagree):

▶ **Answer**

People can recoup⁺ their losses in the stock market, regain a lover's affections (or find a new lover), or reform their character, but they may not ever be able to recover their lost health. However, taking care of ourselves is actually easier than we may think. If we have an adequate, balanced diet, if we get enough rest, and if we pace ourselves⁺ and keep everything in proper perspective⁺ to minimize stress, most of us can maintain our physical activity over a long period (a lifetime!) comfortably and enjoyably. The other really important aspect of staying healthy involves regular exercise. But you don't have to work out⁺ in an expensive gym for several hours a week. A brisk⁺ walk for 30 minutes a day is all most people need, though they may want to supplement this with a few minutes of stretching. Last, but not least, get a thorough medical examination every year. Within days, you will either know that you must take some necessary steps to keep from getting sick, or you will have complete peace of mind knowing that nothing is wrong with you!

Lesson 53
Make Your Point (1)

Make Your point (you may also disagree):

1. * Gas prices are skyrocketing.↓
   * You want to get rid of your car soon.
   * Too many cars are on the road.
   * The subway takes you anywhere
     in the city on time.

2.

   * You want to start taking a lunch box to
     work.
   * You are sick of eating out.
   * Restaurants are too expensive.
   * Too many people dine out, making
     restaurants noisy and uncomfortable.
   * If the restaurant is empty, the food or
     service must be poor.

3. * You think TV can never be educational.
   * It rots↓ a child's brain.
   * Commercials encourage overspending.
   * Children are getting fat from
     watching TV.

4.
* It's amazing how few people seem to be really worried about AIDS.
* AIDS kills you, and it's spreading fast.
* You can get it from engaging in unsafe sex or even getting a blood transfusion.↓
* Most importantly, one must get educated about the disease before it is too late.
* By taking preventive measures, anyone can be safe.

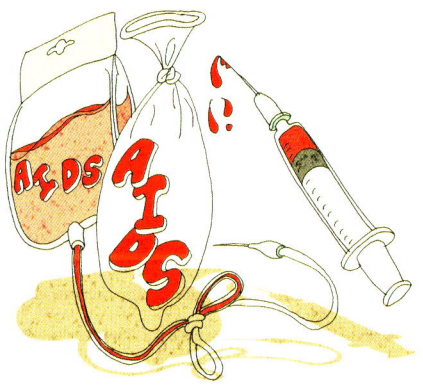

5.

* People are prejudiced↓ against fat people.
* Obesity↓ is a disease.
* Fat people do not just eat whatever they please.
* They have difficulty burning up calories in their everyday activity.
* Even exercise doesn't help some fat people.

6.
* We should make tobacco illegal.
* It is fatal↓ to smokers and nonsmokers alike and poses great risks to people's health.
* Nicotine is among the most addictive of all substances.
* Second-hand smoke can ruin the health even of innocent↓ non-smokers.

Lesson 53
Make Your Point (1)

Make Your point (You may also disagree):

7. * It is true that politicians disgust⁺ us with
their low moral standards.
* People are becoming indifferent⁺ to politics.
* They often neglect to vote.
* The easiest way for evil to triumph⁺ is
for the good to sit back and do nothing.
* We can only stop the vicious circle⁺ of
corrupt politics by voting intelligently.

8. * Stress is unavoidable in modern society.
* We must learn how to cope with it.
If not, we will all be destroyed by it.
* But we can also make it our life's
locomotive.⁺
* If well managed, it stimulates⁺ our
creative power and leads us to
better lives.

9. * Crime rates are on the rise.

* Laws are too permissive.

* Strict punishment is said to discourage criminal acts.

* Singapore is an outstanding example of this theory.

* But the death penalty should be the exception, not the rule.

* Capital punishment is too extreme, given the uncertainties⁺ of the law and police practices.

* No one should be allowed to take a human life — not even a judge.

10. * Some people say life is predetermined before our birth.

* Destiny cannot be changed.

* But we shouldn't be discouraged, because there is something even stronger than fate.

* Good and bad habits are our "real destiny."

* If you choose good habits, your life will be full of light, but bad ones will lead you into darkness.

Book 2
Lesson 54
Make Your Point (2)

▶ **Example**

Why is a college education important?

▶ **Answer**

A college education expands↓ our knowledge of the world, it deepens our interests, it widens our abilities, it makes us more broad-minded↓ and less ignorant,↓ it provides us with useful human contacts, it forces us to work hard to achieve something worthwhile, and, perhaps most importantly, it gives us a certificate↓ (called a diploma) for success.

→**expand :** become larger
→**broad-minded :** willing to respect opinions or behavior that are very different from your own
→**ignorant :** not knowing facts or information that you ought to know
→**certificate :** official document that states facts are true
→**benefit :** (sth) that gives you advantages or improves your life in some way
→**spoil :** damage or ruin

Make your point on the following issues:

1. Why are friends important to us?

2. Why do we have to be on time for appointments?

3. Why is keeping our promises to ourselves the most difficult?

4. Why is it dangerous to drive drunk?

Lesson 54
Make Your Point (2)

Make your point on the following issues:

5. What does having a job mean for you?

6. What is the importance of family?

7. Why are laws necessary?

8. Why are morals necessary?

9. Tell us why we should learn English.

10. What benefits⁺ does money provide?

11. How does money spoil⁺ us?

12. Think of all the reasons why people can't quit drinking and smoking.

Book 2
Lesson 55
Social Phenomena

> ### Example

Juvenile crimes are becoming more prevalent.

> ### Answer

Just a glance at any population chart will show that wherever there are a lot of young men (between their early teens and late 20s), crime rates go up. They constitute a very active force in any society, they have lots of energy and probably too much free time, and they lack maturity. So, unless they have jobs, they are usually on the prowl for something exciting to do, especially something that may make them some money. But they don't usually understand fully the consequences of their actions; they are focused only on short-term thrills or needs.

→ **juvenile :** relating to young people who are not yet adults
→ **prevalent :** common or widespread
→ **constitute :** make up or form (sth)
→ **maturity :** quality of behaving in a sensible way and like an adult
→ **on the prowl :** moving around looking for (sth/sb) in different places
→ **thrill :** sudden strong feeling of excitement and pleasure
→ **on the rise :** increasing
→ **norm :** usual way of doing (sth)
→ **deteriorate :** become worse
→ **life expectancy :** length of time that a person or animal is expected to live
→ **unscrupulous :** behaving in an unfair or dishonest way
→ **upright :** always behaving in an honest way

Make your own point on the following social phenomena:

1. People are almost always busy.

2. Divorce rates are going up too quickly.

3. Family size is much smaller than even 40 years ago.

4. The number of childless couples is on the rise.

Lesson 55
Social Phenomena

Make Your own point on the following social phenomena:

5. More people are driving than ever before.

6. Many people are choosing to remain single longer or not getting married at all.

7. A two-income family is becoming the norm.

8. Almost everybody invests in stocks.

9. Among young people, physical fitness is deteriorating.↓

10. Life expectancy↓ is expanding.

11. No one reads as much as his grandparents did.

12. Dishonest, unscrupulous↓ people are more likely to succeed than the morally upright.↓

Book 2
Lesson 56

Who Is Responsible or Who Is More Responsible?

► **Read ME!**

Let's discuss whether two parties to a dispute are both responsible (and if so, which is more so) or whether only one is.

► **Example**

Today, many angry consumers are suing[↓] tobacco companies for the cost of their smoking-related diseases, especially cancer. They argue that the firms have not educated people enough about the possible consequences of smoking. But the cigarette makers retort[↓] that an adult knows about the harmful effects of smoking and chooses to smoke anyway, so he should be held responsible for his own actions. The company just provides a product but does not force anyone to use it. Do you think smokers are justified in blaming the tobacco companies? Who is more responsible, the smokers or the cigarette makers?

►
→**sue :** make a legal claim against (sb), esp. for money, because they have harmed you in some way
→**retort :** reply quickly, in an angry or humorous reply　　→**hooked :** addicted
→**adjust :** change (sth) in a minor way so that it works better　　→**to the extent :** to the degree
→**trigger :** part of a gun that you press with your finger to fire it
→**the lion's share :** the largest part　　→**determine :** officially decide (sth)
→**at large :** as a whole　　→**at fault :** responsible
→**corrupt :** very bad morally　　→**almighty :** having a great deal of power or importance
→**culpable :** responsible for (sth) bad　　→**liable :** legally responsible
→**cynical :** believing that people are generally selfish and dishonest　　→**naive :** innocent or simple
→**blamed :** responsible　　→**ingrained :** firmly established and therefore difficult to change
→**resent :** feel angry or upset　　→**formality :** formal quality　　→**phony :** false or not real
→**bestow :** give (sb) something of great value or importance

Who is responsible or who is more responsible?

▶ **Answer**

1 Nicotine is one of the most addictive substances known, so, once hooked,⁺ few people can successfully break their smoking habit. Since the companies know this, and even carefully adjust⁺ nicotine levels to maximize sales, they should be held responsible for selling addictive drugs. This is particularly true to the extent⁺ that the firms are marketing to youngsters. People may be blamed because they voluntarily start smoking, but not because they are unable to quit.

2 Whoever begins smoking knows he is holding a gun to his head — is it the tobacco company's fault if he pulls the trigger?⁺ The dangers of smoking, and the difficulties of quitting, are well-known. So the smoker must take the lion's share⁺ of responsibility on himself.

Lesson 56
Who Is Responsible or Who Is More Responsible?

Who is responsible or who is more responsible?

1. Many people say that achieving success is solely a personal matter. They think self-effort is more important than family background or social relationships. On the other hand, some believe that these external factors are all important in determining⁴ how well one does. What do you think? Which is more important: "who you know" or "what you know"?

2.

Too many people are addicted to gambling, drugs, alcohol, etc. Social scientists often claim that society at large⁴ is more responsible than individual victims. Do you think so? If so, then in what way is society at fault?⁴ What role does personal responsibility play, if any?

3. We live in a corrupt⁴ world that is convinced that money has the almighty⁴ power to do anything. Even though bribery is illegal, and givers and takers alike are equally culpable,⁴ the practice continues unabated. Both parties may be liable⁴ to equal punishment, but one question remains unanswered: morally, who is the most responsible, the bribe giver or the bribe taker?

4. We keep electing people to office who promise reforms but, once in office, take full benefit of the same immoral practices they criticized. Who is more responsible for this state of affairs? The cynical* politicians? Or the naive* voters? Or is it the political system itself that should be blamed?*

5. Whether or not sexual discrimination exists in professional life is the subject of a major argument. Some say it does not. But others, especially women, insist that ingrained* social prejudice is at work. If you think unreasonable discrimination against females continues, who do you think is at fault, the men or the women? How can the problem be resolved?

6. Kids show less respect to their elders than they used to. This is a complaint as old as Plato. I suspect that it is mainly a matter of relativity. When we are young, we resent* the formality* and phoniness* that is demanded of us by society. We want to be free and natural, without artificial restraints on our behavior. But, inevitably, we grow older. As we find fewer of our dreams being realized, we want some sign of being important, and we remember what our parents told us about how young people should behave toward older people. We resent not being given the amount of honor we think we are entitled to, but we forget when we were young how little of it we actually bestowed* on others.

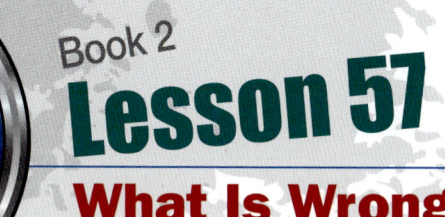

Book 2
Lesson 57
What Is Wrong with This Idea?

Read ME!

Can you discover logical flaws[→] in the way people think?

Example

After long observation he's positive that love in marriage is far less important than a similarity in the couple's wealth and social status.[→]

Answer

Love is an inner quality, not a material property. Love is truest when least deserved and hardest to bestow. Anyone can "love" someone with many pretty objects, an exciting personality, and fantastic looks. But only someone who really loves that individual can joyfully put up with[→] that individual when the fortune is spent, the boredom of middle age has set in, and the body has turned into flab[→] and wrinkles.[→]

→**flaw :** mistake in an argument, plan, or set of ideas
→**status :** your social or professional rank or position, considered in relation to other people
→**put up with :** accept a bad situation or person without complaining; tolerate
→**flab :** extra soft flesh on a person's body
→**wrinkle :** lines on your face or skin that you get when you are old
→**ban :** forbid (sb) from doing (sth)   →**constitute :** make up or form
→**legitimate :** correct, allowable, or operating according to the law
→**obvious :** easy to notice or understand   →**presumably :** very likely
→**outnumber :** be more in number
→**portfolio :** collection of stocks owned by a particular person or company

142

What's wrong with this idea?

1. He claims that street vendors should be banned↓ since they don't pay any taxes, and thus they constitute↓ unfair competition to legitimate↓ businesses.

2. She thinks that spanking our children is a necessary evil if we are to bring them up well. "Spare the rod and spoil the child," she says. Spanking doesn't really hurt any kids, but it helps focus their attention on what they did wrong.

Lesson 57
What Is Wrong with This Idea?

What's wrong with this idea?

3. He believes the more money he had, the happier he would be. If one were only rich, he could do anything, go anywhere, have whatever he wanted. How could any wealthy person fail to be happy?

4. "Since most great leaders have been male, obviously⁺ men are superior to women." At least, that's what my professor says. Maybe he's right. When I try to list great leaders, it's hard to think of any woman at all, but it's always easy to come up with a lot of men.

5. He claims that members of elite society, because they have more money, influence, responsibility, and presumably↓ more ability and intelligence, should have more than one vote. Why should their ability to make good decisions for everyone in the community as a whole be so limited, especially since they are outnumbered↓ by their inferiors, who routinely make bad choices?

6. Parents shouldn't expect their adult offspring to support them. Even if parents have spent a lot of time and money providing for their children's well being, they have merely done their job as parents. Growing kids is a parent's responsibility, and joy; it is not an insurance policy or an investment portfolio.↓

Book 2
Lesson 58
Good Things and Bad

▶ **Example**

All people want to retire early. They want to enjoy their lives comfortably, without having to work. But are they really happy when their dream comes true? What are some good and bad aspects about early retirement?

▶ **Answer**

In my country, I'm eligible⁺ for full retirement at 66, but I can retire early with partial benefits at 62. On the one hand, I'm very tempted⁺ to stop working early. I'm still in good health, and I'd like to travel to many places I haven't had enough time to go to, while I still can. If I wait another four years, my old body might not let me go anywhere. On the other hand, I enjoy my job and, of course, the income that goes with it. I worry that I will have difficulty adjusting⁺ to retirement due to both boredom and bankbook issues. But I guess I have to make up my mind soon, since I'm 61 now.

→**eligible :** able or allowed to do (sth)
→**be tempted to do (sth) :** make (sb) want to have or do (sth)
→**adjust :** gradually get used to a new situation
→**flaunt :** show your money, success, beauty, etc. so that other people notice it
→**status :** social or professional rank or position   →**affluent :** having plenty of money
→**You bet! :** definitely agree   →**subject to :** must obey to
→**conscription:** practice of making people join the military   →**martial :** relating to war or soldiers
→**strain :** cause problems
→**breaking point :** time when a person can no longer accept or deal with a situation because of too much pressure or stress
→**must :** (sth) that is necessary or required

Good things and bad:

1. What kind of car do you like? A compact? A sedan? A sports car? An SUV? Your choice certainly depends on your taste but also, most importantly, on your finances. The rich tend to buy big cars, so they can flaunt↓ their social status↓, while the less affluent↓ must be satisfied with buying compacts. But in most cases you will probably find both satisfaction and dissatisfaction alike, regardless of which type you buy. What are the good things and the bad things about the four kinds of cars?

2. You bet!↓ Young people hate having to be subjected to↓ conscription↓. Many are willing to try every means possible to avoid their military obligations, because they have heard about the hardships and risks. But some, especially the ones who have already finished their military duty, look back and say that they learned many good things and that their lives changed positively as a result. What could they have possibly learned or experienced in the military that would make them feel that way? What other good things and bad things are there about martial↓ life?

Lesson 58
Good Things and Bad

Good things and bad:

3. Remarriage after the death or divorce of a spouse is a very serious problem for many. Doing so may strain↓ existing relationships to the breaking point,↓ especially if children are involved. But it may also be difficult to live alone or even to support oneself or one's family without help. That's why many divorcees choose to remarry. But the problem is that not all of them are happy. What are the good things and bad things about remarriage?

4. I have two uncles. One of them is self-employed, the other one works for a big company. They talk to me about their jobs and try to give me advice. What do you suppose they say about the pluses and minuses of their employment situations?

5. Many people love their dogs and cats as much as they love their children and pay even more attention to them. What are the good and bad things about loving one's pets?

6. Credit cards have become a must↓ in today's economy; some places do not even accept cash anymore. What are the best and worst aspects of having a credit card?

Book 2
Lesson 59
What Has This Change Brought About?

Read ME!

Now is the time to look deeply at how one kind of change brings about other kinds of change, sometimes unexpectedly.

Example

Women's equality in the professional world has meant more than just economic opportunity being available to members of both sexes. What else has it led to?

Answer

Women have a right to pursue their own dreams and interests as much as men do. And clearly many of them are more qualified for their jobs than their male colleagues.↓ But opening the workforce at every level to women has led to many negative consequences as well. For one thing, it has contributed to↓ declining birth rates and exploding↓ divorce rates. For another, it has made it very hard for traditional families, with just one wage earner, to keep up economically and socially with their two-paycheck neighbors.

→**colleague :** (sb) you work with   →**contribute to (sth) :** help make (sth) happen
→**explode :** increasing greatly   →**skyrocket :** increase suddenly and greatly
→**emergence :** act of becoming known or coming into view
→**in its wake :** behind or after it has moved
→**distant :** far away from   →**factor :** (sth) that helps produce or influence a result
→**pose :** be or create (a possible threat, danger, problem, etc.)

What has this change brought about?

1. Skyrocketing⁴ auto ownership has marked Korea's emergence⁴ as a modern consumer society. What changes has the phenomenon brought in its wake?⁴

2. The prevalence of instant food and fast food indicates more convenience for busy people. What else does it cause to change?

Lesson 59
What Has This Change Brought About?

What has this change brought about?

3. The growing number of college graduates rightly indicates that a nation has an adequate pool of highly trained specialists and technicians. What other changes has it caused, though?

4. Living in apartments instead of houses saves spaces, especially in a crowded urban society. But what has been lost due to this particular lifestyle?

5. The Internet means I can easily keep in touch with distant↓ friends, and I can do my work anywhere I happen to be, no matter what time of day it is. But those same factors↓ also contribute to making my life a lot more complicated. In what ways do you think that is true?

6. As societies develop economically, their members tend to work fewer days a week. That's a good thing, I suppose, but it also poses↓ many problems. What do you think some of these might be?

Book 2
Lesson 60
Laughter Is the Best Medicine!

Read ME!

Laugh your way to better health! A vast amount of medical research indicates that laughter produces significant changes in immune system↓ functionality, beginning at the cellular level and pervading↓ the entire biological system. We have long been aware that negative factors, such as depression and stress, can compromise↓ the immune system. But now scientists have clear evidence that laughter can improve it. And the best part about this discovery is that you don't have to wait until you're ill to experience the medical benefits of laughter. Even if you don't laugh much now, you can begin to practice right away. Ready....

→ **immune system :** system that protects your body from diseases and infections
→ **pervade :** spread through all parts of (sth)
→ **compromise :** damage or weaken (sth)
→ **regard :** think of (sb) in a particular way
→ **hand over (sth) :** give up control of (sth)
→ **work :** have the intended effect or result
→ **kidnap :** take (sb) away illegally, usually by force, and demand money for returning them
→ **shed :** release
→ **dock :** place in a court of law where a person who is accused of a crime stands or sits during a trial
→ **starry-eyed :** having hopes and desires that are not realistic or practical
→ **interrupt :** say things while another person is speaking
→ **sympathetic :** feeling or showing concern about (sb) who is in a bad situation
→ **bear :** accept or endure (sth)
→ **shut off :** cause a machine to stop operating; turn off
→ **run off with (sb) :** run away with (sb); disappear with another person, esp. as a way to begin a new relationship

Explain what these jokes mean and comment about them:

▶ **E***xample*

They've been married five years and she still hasn't told him how much money he's earning.

▶ **A***nswer*

The point of the joke is that his wife regards⁺ her husband as a money-making machine, and he seems to accept his destiny as a henpecked hubby, giving her all the money he makes without question or complaint. It's a tragedy that so many husbands hand over⁺ all their money to their wives and then have to beg them for an allowance. Do you think this is a good idea? Or do you think husbands should handle all financial matters themselves? Or would mutual decision making work?⁺

Lesson 60
Laughter Is the Best Medicine!

Explain what these jokes mean and comment about them:

1. He doesn't carry life insurance, only fire insurance — he knows where he's going.

2. My mother-in-law was kidnapped last week. The kidnapper said if we didn't send $25,000 quickly, we would have to take her back.

3. He married his secretary, thinking he'd continue to dictate to her.

4. He's marrying at 70 but is still looking for a home near a school.

5. When he buys anything, he *sees only the initial payment.*

6. They took the "for better or worse" vow, but they didn't say "for how long."

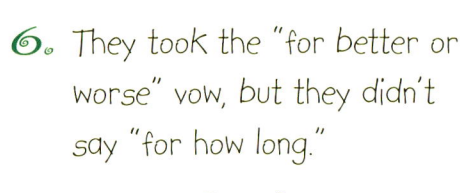

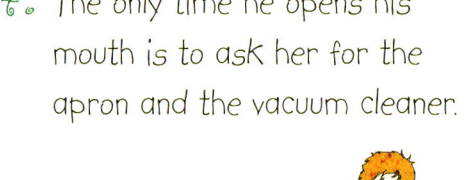

7. The only time he opens his mouth is to ask her for the apron and the vacuum cleaner.

8. She threatened to divorce him once, and he couldn't help shedding* a few cheers.

Lesson 60
Laughter Is the Best Medicine!

Explain what these jokes mean and comment about them:

9. He never knew what happiness was until he married her — then it was too late.

10. Judge to defendant: "I note that in addition to stealing cash, you took watches, rings and pearls." "Yes, your honor," replied the man in the dock.↓ "I was taught that money alone doesn't bring happiness."

11.

"Joe is the man for me," said a starry-eyed↓ young woman to her mother. "He's nice. He's handsome. He's smart. He's hard-working. He's funny. He's strong. He's kind."

"He's married," interrupted↓ her mother. "So? Nobody's perfect!"

12. He told his children Santa Claus is too old to get around anymore.

13. "Father, I want to get married."
"No, my son, you're not wise enough."
"When will I be wise enough?"
"When you rid yourself of the idea that you want to be married."

14.

When he's in, she's out. When she's in, he's out. They can't find each other to discuss a divorce.

Lesson 60
Laughter Is the Best Medicine!

Explain what these jokes mean and comment about them:

15. He could convince his wife that she looks fat in a fur coat.

16. She swore she wouldn't talk to him for a month, and he's certainly unhappy about it — the month is almost over.

17. He's very sympathetic.↓ He can't bear↓ seeing an old lady standing up in the subway, so he always buries his head in a newspaper.

18. As soon as she starts giving her side of the argument, he shuts off↓ his hearing aid.

19. "I've had bad luck with both my wives."
"How come?"
"The first ran off with↓ another man."
"And the second?"
"Didn't."

20.

"My uncle had an automobile accident, but the doctor told him he would have him walking in a month."
"And did he?"
"Yes. When the doctor sent his bill, my uncle had to sell his car to pay it."

LIS KOREA에서 나온
DISCUSSION TEXTBOOK

LIS KOREA는 토론 학습 교재 전문 출판사 입니다.

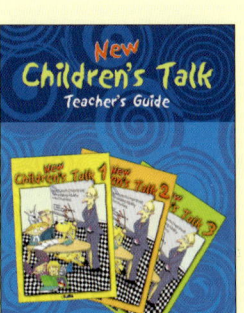

중고급 어린이 들을 위한 독창적인 영어교재

New
Children's Talk(1), (2), (3)

교사용

New
Children's Talk(TG)

- 일상생활에서 벌어지는 상황들을 다양한 포멧에 맞추어서 많은 Speaking Chance를 제공합니다.
- 암기위주의 영어가 아니라 자기의견을 만들어 낼 수 있는 포멧들을 제공합니다.

청소년의 세계와 그들의 생각 관심사들을 토론으로
Chat Room for Teens (1)(2)(3)

- New Children's Talk를 배운 학생들이 Teen Talk를 쉽게 익힐 수 있는 선행학습교재로 사용할 수 있도록 구성
- 학습의 재미와 능률을 높이기 위해 다양한 그림들과 그것들을 바탕으로한 토론들 그리고 실제 많은 상황에서 발생하는 대화들과 수많은 지문들을 바탕으로 토론의 다양성을 확보

LIS KOREA에서 나온
DISCUSSION TEXTBOOK

LIS KOREA는 토론 학습 교재 전문 출판사 입니다.

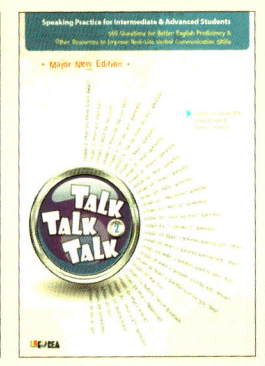

자유토론을 위한 훈련과정
Talk Talk Talk (1), (2)

- Express Yourself/Let's talk/What Do You Think?
  과정을 무리없이 이수하기 위한 예비단계로서 자유토론에 대비하기 위한 많은 훈련과정을 포함하고 있다.
- 여러상황에 맞는 다양한 질문을 학생들에게 던짐으로서 질문과 응답들의 패턴을 이해하고 습득케 하고자 했다.
- Express Yourself/Let's talk/What Do You Think?의 주요 훈련 목표 중 하나인 어떤 영어 단어나 문장을
  토론자 스스로 다시 설명하는 훈련에 중점을 두었다.

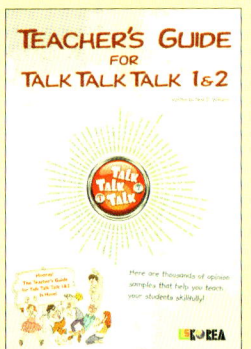

Talk Talk Talk의 선생님 교재
Teacher's Guide for Talk Talk Talk 1&2

- 각권 25개의 이슈와 각 이슈에 대한 다양한 토론주제를 제공하였습니다.
- 토론 주제에 대한 다양한 Opinion Samples를 달아 학습자들에게 도움을 주고자 했습니다.
- 각각의 이슈마다 그와 연관된 Dialogue를 첨부하여 학습자들이 다양한 구어체의 표현을 익히도록
  했습니다.

LIS KOREA에서 나온
DISCUSSION TEXTBOOK

LIS KOREA는 토론 학습 교재 전문 출판사 입니다.

중고급 토론교재의 결정판
LET'S TALK! (1), (2)

- 실생활과 아주 밀접하고 분명한 의견 대립이 나올수 있는 주제를 선정 고급 토론 영어를 위한 기초를 가질 수 있도록 구성.
- 토론 영어의 기초 단계인 영어로 설명하는 힘을 길러주기 위해 "What Does It Mean?"을 삽입.

- Question에서는 제시된 주제에 대한 이해력 측정뿐만 아니라 한 주제에 대한 깊이있는 토론에 대비하는 힘을 길러 주고자 했다.
- Discussion Points에서는 주어진 주제에 대한 토론 포인트는 물론이고 그와 연관된 많은 주제 제공
- Opinion Samples에서는 학습자들이 주어진 주제에 대해 토론을 준비할 수 있도록 만은 찬반 의견과 참고 의견들을 제시하고 있다.
- 어려운 표현이나 Idiomatic Expressions에 대해 각주에 충분한 영어 설명을 달아 학습자들로 하여금 이해가 쉽도록 하였다.

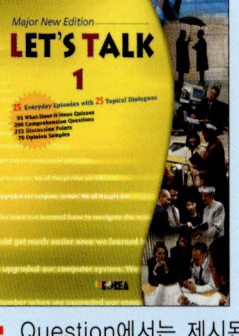 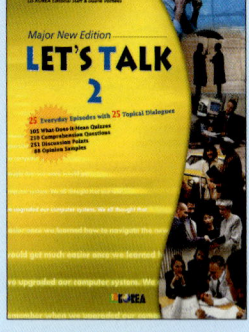

중급자들을 위한 토론교재
SPEAK YOUR MIND (1) (2)

- 일상적이며 쉬운 주제들을 선정하여 간결하게 정리했음.
- 대표 주제에 대한 질문과 대답을 여론조사 형식으로 꾸며 독자들이 쉽게 주제에 접근할 수 있도록 했음.
- 모든 주제들에 찬반의견을 달아 독자들의 다양한 의견을 접할 수 있도록 했음.

LIS KOREA 에서 나온
DISCUSSION TEXTBOOK

LIS KOREA 는 토론 학습 교재 전문 출판사 입니다.

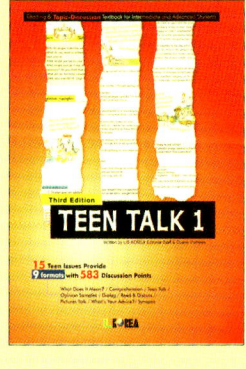
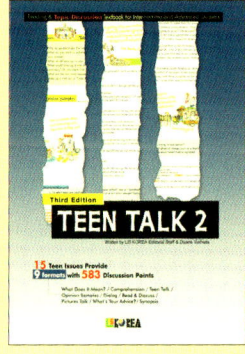

청소년을 위한 토론교재
New Teen Talk (1), (2)

- 청소년 토론교재의 최고 높은 단계의 교재로서 각권 15개의 이슈속에 500개 이상의 토론주제를 제시 합니다.
- 각 권에 포함된 9개의 포멧은 (What Does It Mean? / Comprehension/ Teen Talk / Opinion Samples / Dialog / Read& Discuss/ Pictures Talk / What's Your Advice? /Synopsis/) 각각의 특징에 맞는 다양하고 흥미로운 토론 주제를 제공합니다.

설명간결한 형식의 새로운 토론교재
Express Yourself Directly (1), (2)

- Pictures Talk 섹션에서는 큰 주제에 대한 warm-up 주제들을 선정하여 그림 과 함께 제시하여 본주제에 쉽게 접근할 수 있도록 했습니다.
- Express Yourself Directly 섹션에서는 Pictures Talk 섹션에서 다루지 않은 좀더 깊은 주제를 선정하여 심도있는 토론이 되도록 했습니다.
- Let's Talk Funny 섹션에서는 본 주제와 관련있는 재미있는 이야기를 실어 가벼운 토론과 함께 긴장을 풀도록 했습니다.

- What Does It Mean?에서는 본 주제와 관련된 Food For Thought를 제공하여 학습자들이 자유롭게 토론 할수 있도록 했으면 다양한 의견이 나올 수 있는 문구 들을 제시하였습니다.
- 마지막으로 Synopsis에서는 (전체 400의 그림으로 구성) 각 그림에 대한 설명을 영어로 명쾌하게 제시 하여 학습자로 하여금 주제에 대한 최종 복습을 할 수 있도록 했습니다.

LIS KOREA 에서 나온
DISCUSSION TEXTBOOK

LIS KOREA 는 토론 학습 교재 전문 출판사 입니다.

본격적인 비지니스 토론 교재
LET'S TALK BUSINESS

- 20개의 현대 비즈니스 주제가 78개의 Talking Points를 제공합니다.
- 수 백 개의 다양한 어휘와 표현들이 예문과 함께 어우러져 Self-study를 가능하게 합니다.
- 20개의 Topical Dialogue별도 수록

재미있는 창작 이야기로 토론의 즐거움을
LET'S TALK FUNNY

- 70개의 재미있는 창작 이야기가 수 백 개의 토론 이슈와 어우러져 독자들에게 재미있게 영어로 토론 할 수 있는 기회를 제공합니다.
- 또한 우리생활에 감추어져 있던 또 다른 50개의 Thinking Points를 제공하여 발상을 전환할 수 있는 계기가 되도록 했습니다.

LIS KOREA 에서 나온
DISCUSSION TEXTBOOK

LIS KOREA 는 토론 학습 교재 전문 출판사 입니다.

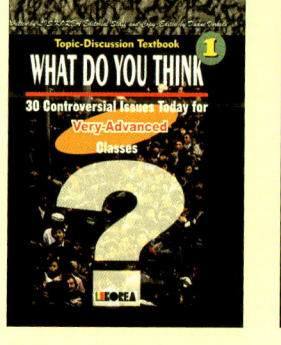
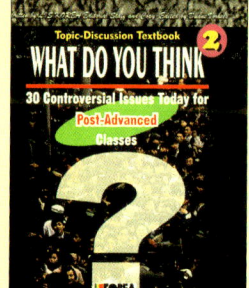

고급 토론 교재의 완결판
What Do You Think? (1), (2)

- Let's talk를 끝낸 학습자들이 좀더 시사적이며 깊이있는 문제들에 대해 토론할 수 있도록 구성
- 토론 영어의 기초단계인 영어로 설명하는 힘을 길러 주기 위해 What Does It Mean?을 삽입
- Question에서는 제시된 주제에 대한 이해력 측정 뿐만 아니라 한 주제에 대한 깊이있는 토론에 대비 하는 힘을 길러 주고자 했다.

- What Do You Think?에서는 주어진 주제에 대한 토론 포인트는 물론이고 그와 연관된 많은 주제 제공
- Opinion Samples에서는 학습자들이 주어진 주제에 대해 토론을 준비할 수 있도록 만은 찬반의견과 참고 의견들을 제시하고 있다.
- 어려운 표현이나 Idiomatic Expressions에 대해 각주에 충분한 영어 설명을 달아 학습지들로 하여금 이해가 쉽도록 하였다.

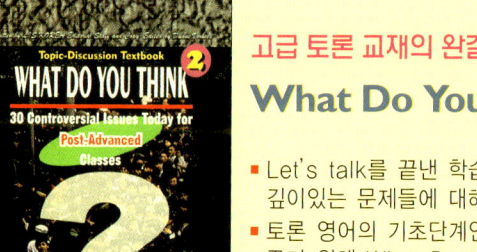

토론교재의 베스트셀러
EXPRESS YOURSELF (1), (2)

- 각권 25개의 이슈와 각 이슈에 대한 다양한 토론주제를 제공하였습니다.
- 토론 주제에 대한 다양한 Opinion Samples를 달아 학습자들에게 도움을 주고자 했습니다.
- 각각의 이슈마다 그와 연관된 Dialogue를 첨부하여 학습자들이 다양한 구어체의 표현을 익히도록 했습니다.

Talk Talk Talk ②

초판 5쇄 인쇄 : 2017년 10월 1일 인쇄
초판 5쇄 발행 : 2017년 10월 5일 발행
지 은 이 : 리스코리아 편집부
          & Duane Vorhees
일러스트레이터 : 김기환
편 집 디 자 인 : 예림칼라
펴 낸 곳 : (도서출판) 리스코리아
펴 낸 이 : 조은예
등   록 : 남양주 제 399-2011-000003호
전   화 : (0502) 423-7947
팩   스 : (0303) 3447-7947

www.liskorea.co.kr

All rights reserved. No part of this book may be
reproduced, stored in a retrieval system, or
transmitted in any form or by any means, electronic,
mechanical, photocopying, recording or otherwise,
without the prior permission in writing of the Publisher.